How To Make a Bulb Garden
With Planting Tables For Bulbs

by The Countryside Press
of Harrisburg, Pennsylvania

with an introduction by Roger Chambers

This work contains material that was originally published in 1915.

This publication was created and published for the public benefit, utilizing public funding and is within the Public Domain.

This edition is reprinted for educational purposes and in accordance with all applicable Federal Laws.

Introduction Copyright 2017 by Roger Chambers

COVER CREDITS

Front Cover
Dahlia Pinnata by *Juni* from Kyoto, Japan (Flickr.com)
[CC BY 2.0 (http://creativecommons.org/licenses/by/2.0)],
via Wikimedia Commons

Back Cover
Snowdrops by *Orangeaurochs* from Sandy, Bedfordshire, United Kingdom
[CC BY 2.0 (http://creativecommons.org/licenses/by/2.0)],
via Wikimedia Commons

Research / Sources
Wikimedia Commons
www.Commons.Wikimedia.org

Many thanks to all the incredible photographers, artists,
researchers, and archivists who share their great work.

PLEASE NOTE :
As with all reprinted books of this age that are intended to perfectly reproduce the original edition, considerable pains and effort had to be undertaken to correct fading and sometimes outright damage to existing proofs of this title. At times, this task can be quite monumental, requiring an almost total rebuilding of some pages from digital proofs of multiple copies. Despite this, imperfections still sometimes exist in the final proof and may detract slightly from the visual appearance of the text.

DISCLAIMER :
Due to the age of this book, some methods or practices may have been deemed unsafe or unacceptable in the interim years. In utilizing the information herein, you do so at your own risk. We republish antiquarian books without judgment or revisionism, solely for their historical and cultural importance, and for educational purposes.

Self Reliance Books

Get more historic titles on animal and stock breeding, gardening and old fashioned skills by visiting us at:

http://selfreliancebooks.blogspot.com/

introduction

I am very pleased to present to you another wonderful old book on horticulture – *How To Make a Bulb Garden*. It was written by *The Countryside Press* of Harrisburg, Pennsylvania, and first published in 1915, making it over a century old.

Due to the public's increased interest in growing and producing various things – from their own food to flowers for cutting, to rearing their own animals for meat, and raising chickens for eggs, we've dedicated ourselves to bringing you the best in dusty-old-book knowledge.

Basic skills like the ability to grow a flower garden, plant a veggie patch, or even some fruit trees have waned over the last century. But there has been a renaissance in the last few years and so many people want to learn these skills again.

We hope these books will be an inspiration to you and help you rediscover simple pleasures like growing you own flowers for cutting, to fill you home with their uplifting colors and fragrance all through the seasons.

The book covers topics like *Good Named Bulbs, Where To Plant, Naturalizing Bulbs, Spring Beginnings, Old-Fashioned Dahlias, The Gladioli, How To Plant, The Elephant's Ear, Tulips For Display*, and more. Also features bulb planting tables.

A short, but knowledgeable old book, perfect for all bulb-growers and flower-growing enthusiasts.

~ *Roger Chambers*

State of Jefferson, December 2017

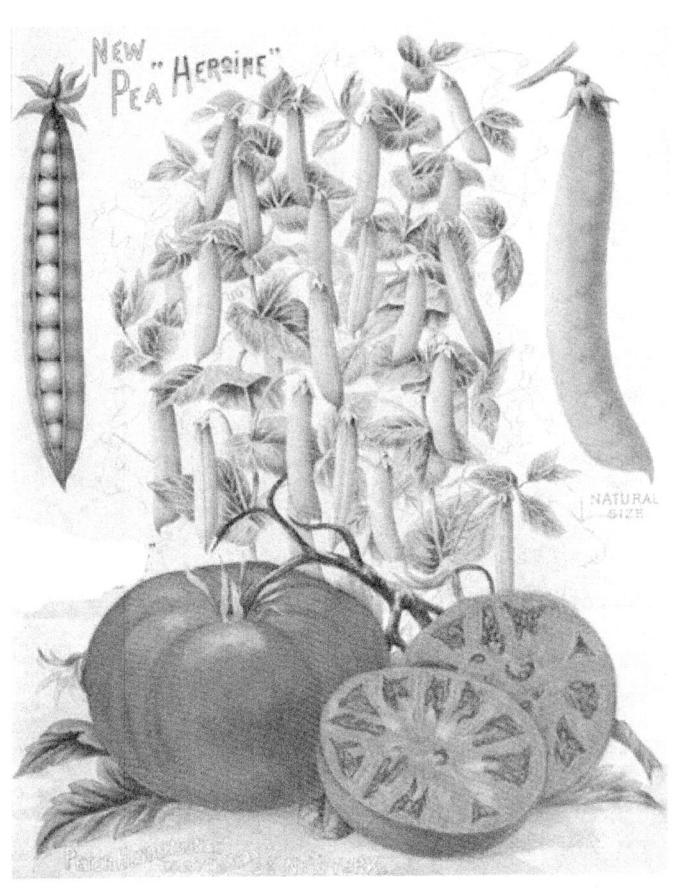

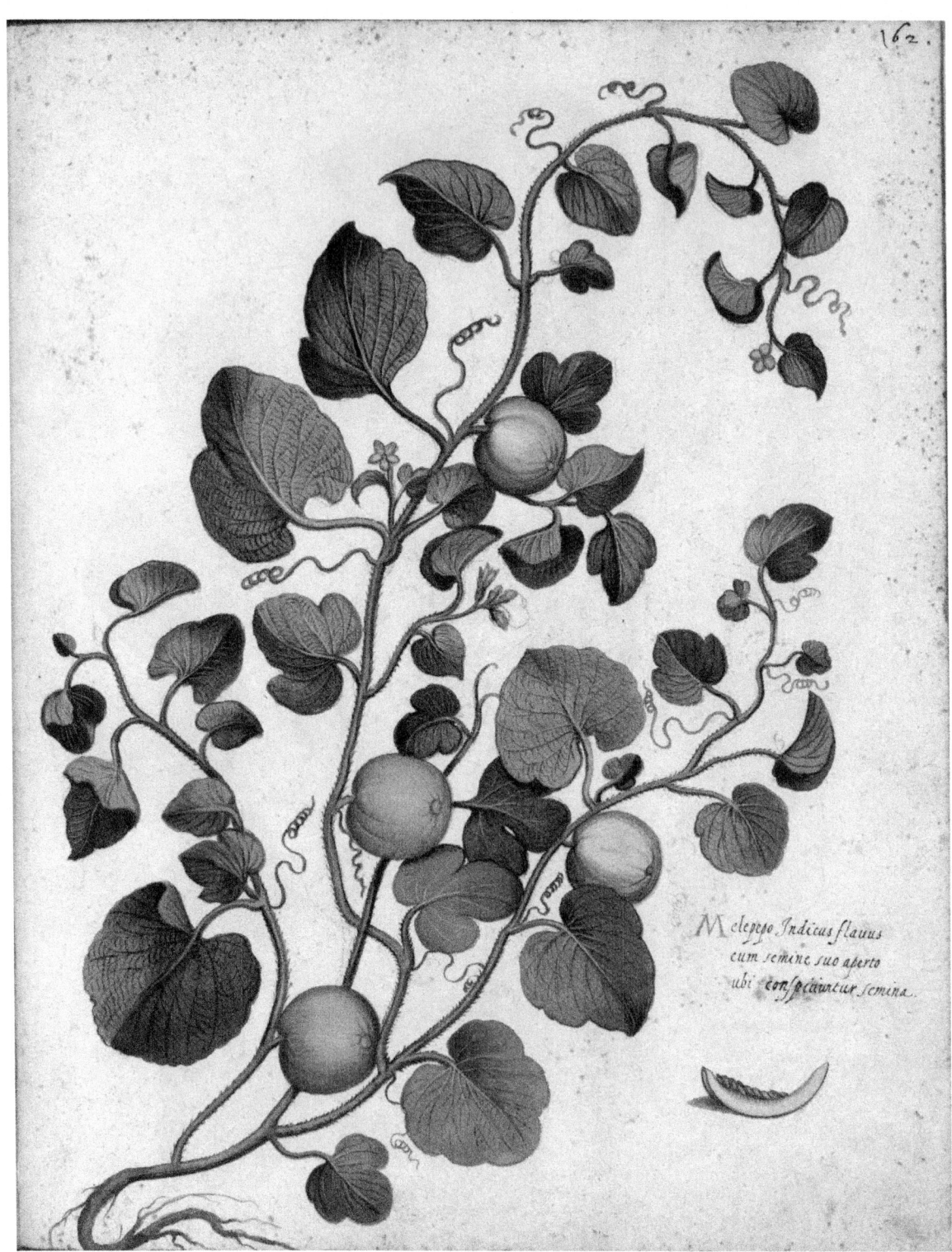

Tulips in the garden border

TABLE OF CONTENTS

	PAGE
Introduction	9
Good Named Bulbs	12
Where to Plant	14
Naturalizing Bulbs	16
Early Bloomers	18
Spring Beginnings	20
The Cheerful Cannas	22
Old-fashioned Dahlias	23
The Gladioli	26
How to Plant	29
Favorite Varieties	30
The Fragrant Tuberose	33
The Elephant's Ear	34
Tigridias	34
Fall-planted Bulbs	35
Tulips for Display	36
Formal Beds	38
Depths to Plant	42
Time to Plant	43
Select Lists	44
Exhibition Hyacinths	44
Single Early Tulips	46
Double Tulips	47
Late Tulips	47
Darwin Tulips	48
Narcissi	49
Jonquils	50
Polyanthus Narcissi	50
Hyacinths	50
Lilies to the Front	51
The Madonna Lily	52
Other Good Lilies	55
Some "Near" Lilies	56
Cultural Requirements	58
A Special Bulb-garden	58
Miscellaneous Bulbs	59
Several Good Qualities	61
Paths and Beds	62
Details of Planting	64
Planting Tables	66–73

INTRODUCTION

THERE have been compiled, within the covers of this little book, the essential things which the amateur should know in connection with obtaining the best results from the planting of bulbs. Much of this material has appeared previously in Suburban Life, but the condensed form in which it is now published will render it still more valuable, as all but the essential facts have been eliminated.

Both spring-flowering and summer-blooming bulbs are included, and plain, concise directions given for their treatment—directions which are easily followed by one even without any previous experience in gardening.

This little book is made possible by the permission of The Suburban Press, and is offered to the garden-lover in the hope it may prove a valuable handbook on the subject of bulb-planting.

THE PUBLISHERS.

HOW TO MAKE A BULB-GARDEN

FIRST in all the garden list for the roaming American suburbanite stand the hardy bulbs—the "Dutch bulbs," as they are often called because so many of them are produced in Holland. They are hardy and lusty, prompt and ready, incomparably showy, and not expensive. Does the new lease-holder in a suburb, or even one in a city, who has a bit of garden, want to have something for immediate effect?—something to make his garden pretty and home-like the very first spring? The final reply to all his questions is tulips. Or at most it is tulips and crocuses and narcissi and a few other Dutch bulbs.

The bulbous plants—tulip, hyacinth, narcissus, crocus, snowdrop, etc.,—produce the earliest showy flowers outdoors in the spring, and October is the month in which to prepare for this floral display. There are many ways that they can be used with telling effect, such as borders to walks, long, narrow beds around the house next to the foundation, beds in the lawn, as clumps in the hardy border or at the front of plantations of shrubbery, or, in the case of the daffodils or narcissi, snowdrops, crocuses and similar bulbs, for naturalizing in the lawn or open woodland.

GOOD NAMED BULBS

To insure that the display will be good, buy the best bulbs that can be secured, and buy named varieties. Mixed lots of many kinds may be bought, but they have the distinct disadvantage of presenting, when in bloom, a heterogeneous mass of colors which is not wanted, particularly in the case where they are used for bedding purposes. Another drawback to mixed lots is that they will not all bloom at the same time. When named varieties are bought, the exact shades of colors wanted for any particular bed can be selected, in varieties that will bloom at the same time. These can be picked from any of the bulb merchants' catalogues, for most of them indicate the comparative blooming date of each variety.

It is important that some attention be given this detail, otherwise disappointment is sure to follow next spring, when the flowers are in bloom.

One spring I walked over the grounds of a large public institution that had extensive bulb-plantings, and to which no attention had been paid as to the flowering season of the varieties in each bed. There were beds of hyacinths in which part were in full bloom, while in the balance of the bed the flower-spikes had just come through the ground. When the second lot was in full bloom, the first to bloom had turned brown and were exceedingly unsightly,—a condition that could have been avoided by a little careful selection on the part of the gardener.

Dutch hyacinths in a set bed

If you have taken pains to get varieties that bloom at the same time, you may be disappointed in their not blooming at the same time, if careless planting methods are adopted. In order that the bulbs will bloom at the same time, they must all be planted at the same depth.

WHERE TO PLANT

All of the spring-flowering bulbs may be planted in almost any situation about the grounds, even though it be quite shaded, and they will bloom; but for the most of them a sunny situation is to be preferred. The daffodils, on the other hand, prefer a partially shaded situation,—not too dense a shade, the force of the rays of the sun need only be broken. Ideal locations for naturalizing the daffodils are in orchards, along the banks of ponds and streams, and among the shrubbery, while the crocus and snowdrop find a congenial place in the lawn.

Almost any soil that is rich will produce good spikes of flowers from good bulbs. You must buy good bulbs to get good spikes, for the number of flowers is entirely controlled by the culture they received in the bulb-gardens. The tulips and hyacinths prefer a well-drained and slightly sandy soil, while the daffodils and other narcissi succeed better in a rather heavy soil.

Many of the bulb catalogues have a little diagram that tells at a glance at what depth to plant the different kinds of bulbs. Detailed information

HOW TO MAKE A BULB-GARDEN 15

about this can also be secured from the planting table in the back part of this book.

That the bulbs may make the best possible growth, the soil should be rich; but if manure must be added just previous to planting, as will be necessary if the beds have contained flowering plants during the summer, spade the manure in deep enough so that it will not come in contact with the bulbs.

Crocuses in the grass

The best way to make a bulb-bed, especially where manure must be added, is to dig it out an inch deeper than the required depth of planting. Spade in the manure, stirring the soil to the depth of about fourteen inches below the original surface of the soil, leveling it off carefully; or, if the surface of the bed when completed is to be crowned, crown this surface and spread half an inch of sand over it. Then set the bulbs where they are to grow, and cover them with the soil taken out. The manure is mixed with the soil under the sand, but that which is on top does not contain any.

A quicker method is that of making holes with a dibble; but, if this is done, there is always an uncertainty of not getting them all at the same depth, and care must be taken that the bulb is not "hung" in the hole; that is, the hole gets too deep and there is a space below the base of the bulb. To avoid this, fill the bottom of the hole with sand, or fine soil, and press the bulb into it to the required depth.

A long, narrow trowel is better than a dibble, but be sure of getting the holes all dug the same depth. The best plan is to dig all the holes before planting any of the bulbs.

NATURALIZING BULBS

By "naturalizing" bulbs is meant the planting of them in out-of-the-way places, where the grass is not mowed closely, amongst the shrubs and perennials, where they will not be disturbed, and where

HOW TO MAKE A BULB-GARDEN 17

they can continue to grow and bloom year after year just as if Nature had placed them there, or in clumps about the lawn. In this way they virtually become "wild" flowers, and, like other wild flowers, repeat their message of joy each spring.

For naturalizing bulbs, planting with a dibble is necessary, for only one bulb is planted at a time.

Poet's narcissus along a stream-bank

The best way to distribute bulbs in a sod is to take several in the hand and throw them at the locality where they are wanted, giving them a whirling motion as they leave the hand; this will prevent the bulbs from being planted in straight lines or geometrical forms, if each is planted where it falls.

The narcissi and daffodils are the best of the larger-flowering bulbs for naturalizing, and they cost from one dollar a hundred up, according to the variety bought. The cheapest form is one of the varieties of the poet's narcissus, Recurvis. It costs only about one dollar a hundred, and Ornatus, another good variety, can be had for a dollar and a half. Many kinds may be secured for two to three dollars a hundred. Emperor is one of the best, costing, in lots of a hundred or more, only about three cents apiece, and Empress is another excellent one for the same price.

EARLY BLOOMERS

In our desire for those flowers which, by their size and color, make the garden brilliant in early spring, we are apt to overlook the smaller kinds, which really bring to us the first indication that Nature is awaking from her winter sleep.

Among these is the snowdrop, with its dainty bells of pure white, which sometimes can be found peeping through a light covering of snow. This is a delightful flower for edging the beds of the larger bulbs, and, with the charming blue and white bells of the chionodoxa, or glory-of-the-snow, makes a most happy combination.

The crocus, too, is a flower which should be grown in all bulb-gardens, and can be used with good effect in solid beds, mixed with other bulbs, or naturalized in the lawn. For this use, turn up a small piece of sod with a trowel and place the bulbs under it. They will bloom and be out of the way when it is time to use the lawn mower.

Tulips and hyacinths are the best of the bulbous plants for bedding, and, of the two, the tulip has always been the more satisfactory.

Unnamed hyacinths, mixed as to varieties, but all of one color, may be had for five or six dollars a hundred, but the best bedding hyacinths, named so that you know just what the shade of blue, pink or other color is, can be purchased for six to eight or nine dollars a hundred. These are to be preferred, as better color combinations can be made with them.

For a bed about 7 feet long and 3½ feet wide,

The dainty snowdrop

ninety-eight hyacinths will be needed. An oval bed 11 x 8 will need about three hundred bulbs.

The first tulips to come into bloom are the Duc Van Thols, followed by the common bedding tulips, and the season is finished by the Cottage Garden and Darwin tulips.

A circular bed of tulips, 6 feet in diameter, will need about three hundred bulbs, if planted 4 inches apart; a bed 6 feet square will need 375 bulbs. Of the common bedding tulips, I prefer Keizerkroon, a tulip of medium height, 15 to 18 inches, with a large, crimson-scarlet flower edged with yellow. They cost only about two and one-half dollars a hundred, and they make a beautiful display.

SPRING BEGINNINGS

The main plantings of Dutch bulbs are made in October or November, but as it is always easier to begin gardening in the spring season, we will adopt that order for the present book. There are a number of bulbous plants which may be planted at any time in May after the danger of frosts has passed, and which will give satisfactory returns as bedding plants or in the way of cut-flowers. The bulbs are cheap; they may be lifted in the fall, and stored over winter and planted out the following summer, and there will be more bulbs to plant the second year because of the natural increase.

The most commonly used bulbous plant for summer decoration is the canna, which is easily grown, produces good mass effects, even when not in flower, and is inexpensive. Bulbs already started or field-grown roots,—clumps of bulbs just as they were dug up in the fall,—may be bought from the

Canna-bed for color

florists or seedsmen. Started bulbs will give quicker effects than the field-grown roots, but the latter are cheaper. When buying these field-grown roots, it is necessary to divide them, being careful that each bulb has a piece of the woody stem which contains buds; otherwise the roots will not produce new plants.

THE CHEERFUL CANNAS

There is a wide choice among cannas; they may be had at varying heights, from 1½ to 6 feet, and

The modern cactus dahlia

they will bear a profusion of red or yellow flowers. The orchid-flowered canna has very large and beautifully shaped blossoms, the petals being unusually broad.

The foliage of the canna also differs; while ordinarily green, there are varieties with deep bronze-colored leaves.

Next to the canna, the dahlia is, perhaps, the most popular of the bulbous plants which may be planted in the spring; it is not, however, nearly so good as a bedding plant. It may be used in the border, among shrubbery, or planted out by itself in the back garden to produce cut-flowers, and the latter use is really the best to which the dahlia can be put, for, after it once commences flowering in summer, it usually continues until frost kills the tops. There is a wide range of color among dahlia flowers, from white to dark red. There is also great variety in shapes; there is the single dahlia, which looks like a large, broad-leaved, colored daisy having very broad florets, the cactus dahlia, and the show dahlia, the latter having the appearance of a big, fluted ball.

OLD-FASHIONED DAHLIAS

One may buy young plants, but this is really unnecessary, as in the eastern United States early-started dahlias seldom give the same returns to the grower as late-started bulbs, for the dahlia will not bloom successfully in the excessively hot summer weather to which localities from New York south-

The formal show dahlia

ward are subject. North of New York, the dahlia will flower much better during the summer. Bulbs set in the ground any time in May after all danger of frost is past, however, will give satisfaction in most localities. In the hotter climates, they should not be planted until about the first of June.

Recently there has been an entirely new race of

HOW TO MAKE A BULB-GARDEN

dahlias produced by crossing the common kind with a newly discovered Mexican species. The flowers of this new race of dahlias are produced on much longer stems than the ordinary dahlia, which makes it very desirable as cut-flowers, for one does not have to cut off flower-buds in order to get long stems, as

Collarette dahlia—an odd variety

is the case with the dahlias with which we are familiar. This new dahlia is particularly desirable because its large crop of flowers is produced before the fall frosts arrive.

THE GLADIOLI

The third important bulb for planting in May is the gladiolus, which is more hardy than the canna or the dahlia, so it may be planted even when there

How new bulbs are formed

is still danger of a few frosts. On account of the stiff character of the gladiolus, it does not make a good bedding plant, unless there is an edging of some low-growing plant.

The bulbs should be planted 2 inches deep and 4 to 5 inches apart, and if to be used for bedding purposes the rows should be a little farther apart, say 10 inches, so that in two or three weeks another planting may be made between the original rows. This will insure a succession of bloom up to the time

The stately gladiolus

the frosts come. There is a wide diversity of color in the flowers, and the gladiolus increases rapidly. Each year, upon digging up the bulbs, a lot of bulblets will be found around the base of the plant, some only one-quarter of an inch in diameter. If all of them are removed in the spring and planted in rows in the garden, they will make plants which will flower the following year. They are very easily removed, it only being necessary to rub them off with the finger.

GOOD GLAD GLADIOLI

Rightly named is the gladiolus, as it makes us glad almost the whole year. Are we not glad from the time when the eagerly looked-for package arrives from the florist's, and we almost reverently lift the fresh, plump bulbs from their wrappings, and speculate upon their possibilities? The variety and unrivaled brilliancy of their colors, together with the ease with which they may be grown, and the variety of conditions under which they thrive, are reasons why these bulbs should be grown in every garden. We are glad again when the light green points begin breaking through the soil, because we know that every bulb planted will be sure to yield one or more lovely flower-spikes.

It is doubtful if any flower can be grown in our gardens that will give greater satisfaction than a bed of gladioli. It seems no exaggeration to say that, for real refined beauty and general usefulness, they stand unrivaled among the many lovely summer-blooming bulbs.

My collection was started with one hundred bulbs—Groff's mixed hybrids. Every season, I add a few of some named variety. Sometimes I buy only one or two of the newer and more expensive sorts. These new ones are always planted by themselves, so that they may receive a little extra care, and give me an opportunity to become thoroughly acquainted with their characteristics. If I am much pleased with them, the bulbs are carefully lifted in the fall and stored during the winter in dry sand, to prevent the bulblets, which form on the old bulb, drying out. By keeping up my experiments in this way I always have the best.

HOW TO PLANT

In the spring, these little bulbs are planted about an inch deep in a box of light, rich soil, and placed out where they get the morning sun. If the bulblets are peeled, they will come up in a few days. Before I knew this little secret, I planted them with their jackets on. But few came up, and those only after weeks of waiting. Of course, they did not amount to much, and for several years the little offsets were thrown away. Now I save the bulblets from my choice varieties, as I find they will come up in about ten days, and make blooming-size bulbs for the next season, some of them over an inch in diameter

One season, I tried two bulbs of the new ruffled type of gladiolus, Glory. It is, indeed, a lovely flower. The bulbs gave four large, strong stalks, with broadly expanded flowers of a light peachy tint or pinkish white, with ruffled edges which add much to their beauty. When lifted, I found that each bulb had produced two fully as large again as the ones planted, with dozens of bulblets.

FAVORITE VARIETIES

Another charming one is Mrs. Francis King, an unusually vigorous, strong-growing sort. The flowers are nearly 5 inches in diameter, a mingling of dazzling scarlet and crimson. They make a wonderful display in the garden, as so many flowers are open at one time. They are also very brilliant under artificial light. The only reason this bulb is so cheap is because it multiplies rapidly, the flower being fully as hand-

Flower-spikes of the Gladiolus in the border

some as, and more showy than, Princeps, which seldom has more than two flowers open at one time, and which, with me, has never increased.

America and Blue Jay are two very beautiful varieties. America, a bright pink, is too well known to need any description. Blue Jay is usually conceded to be the best of the blues. Personally, I am very partial to all of the pansy-colored sorts. They are not so frequently seen as the older varieties, and are sure to attract attention. They appear to best advantage in a vase by themselves, or with only white or yellow colors.

Canary-Bird, Klondyke, Eldorado, and Sulphur King are all good yellows. Snowbank and Augusta are among the cheapest, as well as the best, of the whites. Augusta has a medium-sized flower of pure white, with blue anthers. The stalk is tall and straight, with usually two branches. This sort increases rapidly. If you like a bold, striking flower, you should plant Mephistopheles. This combination of scarlet, black and yellow is sure to attract attention.

The gladiolus has been separated into classes according to color, and may be bought in shades of white and light, striped and variegated, pink and rose, red and scarlet, yellow and orange, and blue hybrids. A good way to obtain a fine collection is to buy twenty-five of each class, which may be obtained at the hundred rates. Considerable taste and endless study are required, however, to make these color schemes succeed.

PROPER SOILS

The gladiolus may be planted in any soil that will grow good vegetables, but prefers a moist loam, in full sunshine. The bulbs should be set from 4 to 6 inches deep, according to the soil. Shallow-planted bulbs will need some support, which should be given early. I grow most of mine in the vegetable garden for cutting. The bulbs are planted 5 inches deep in double rows, 6 inches apart in the row, but 15 inches is allowed between the double rows. As soon as they are up, cultivation begins and is kept up all summer.

I find one planting, the latter part of May, to be all that is necessary. Almost before we know it, the flower-stalk appears, and all summer and fall great quantities of flowers may be cut, equally useful as a table or parlor decoration, or a bride's bouquet. Combined with ferns, the gladiolus forms a beautiful offering for the casket or grave of a loved one.

The bulbs should be left in the ground until danger of frost appears, when they should be carefully lifted (not pulled up) and spread in a warm, dry place for a few days, after which the stalk is cut off about 2 inches from the bulbs. They are then placed in baskets, and hung from the ceiling in the cellar. There is never any question about their keeping.

The gladiolus bulb blossoms but once, and, while producing the foliage and floral spike, another or new bulb develops on top of the old one from which it

HOW TO MAKE A BULB-GARDEN 33

must be detached. At the same time numerous tiny bulblets are formed, the replanting of which matures them the second year. Surely, a flower so easy to grow, so reasonable in price, so decorative, and so much admired, should be grown by everyone who has a foot of land.

THE FRAGRANT TUBEROSE

The most fragrant bulbous flower grown in the garden is the tuberose. The odor is so powerful that some people object to it; but a few plants grown in a corner of the garden will lend a charm that can be imparted in no other way. There are two kinds, tall and short, the tall kinds have stems 2 feet or

Tuberose

over, while the dwarf variety seldom grows over 18 inches high. Bulbs planted late in May will produce flowers in August. There is, however, a somewhat earlier-blooming variety, Albino, which flowers during July. It is single, and the odor is not so powerful, a fact which recommends it to those who object to the stronger odor of the common kind.

THE ELEPHANT'S EAR

One plant which often creates much rivalry among neighbors, who try to see who can grow the biggest leaf, is the elephant's ear (caladium). Bulbs of this plant may be purchased and planted out just as soon as all danger of frost is passed, and, if the soil is moist and rich, large leaves of deep green will be produced. It is impossible to give the elephant's ear too much food. Mulch the soil about it with 4 or 5 inches of well-decayed manure; if the summer is dry give the soil frequent soakings.

TIGRIDIAS

The showiest of all the bulbous plants which one may plant out-of-doors in the spring is the shell flower (tigridia). It has flowers 2 or more inches across, yellow, orange, or purplish, that are variously spotted. The tigridia blooms in July and August. Pavonia is a common species, but it has many varieties. It needs the same treatment exactly as the gladiolus.

Showy tigridias

FALL-PLANTED BULBS

After all, the main show of spring bulbs is provided for by fall planting. These are the tulips, narcissi, hyacinths, etc. Most of the leading dealers issue special autumn catalogues for these goods, and every garden-owner will surely want to see that seductive literature.

One of the most difficult things for the beginner to decide is just what kind of bulbs to get. Sometimes the pocketbook is limited, or the space for planting is small; in either case, it is difficult to know what to buy, in order to obtain the best results from the money expended, and the space of ground at the disposal of the planter.

It is also difficult to advise the planter without knowing all the circumstances. Some who have a dollar to spend would like to buy everything. They look through the catalogues at the great variety of good things offered and become confused, and finally end by buying a dozen or fifteen different varieties with their dollar. This is a mistake. A person who has only one dollar to spend ought to buy a very few varieties, but as many of each variety as possible. When bought by the dozen, an average of about thirty bulbs can be had for the above sum of money; whereas, if single bulbs are purchased the average number would be only fifteen for the same amount.

TULIPS FOR DISPLAY

One tulip in the garden will attract attention, but only because it contrasts with the other objects around it, and it looks too much like a lone sentinel to be effective. One dozen will attract attention because of their own exquisite beauty; while one hundred will make a man wake up and take notice, unless he is indifferent to the grander sights of earth. The number of varieties may be added to from year to year, and, when properly taken care of, the natural increase will, in a few years, make a large and magnificent display.

A group of Keizerkroon tulips

Formal bedding is the fashionable way of planting tulips and hyacinths today, although to the writer's mind there is nothing more delightfully pleasant to the senses than the careless mingling of the various colors which belong to these flowers. A bed of mixed tulips, with their scarlet, vermilion and gold, orange, rose and white, or the kaleidoscopic blending of rose, cream, crimson, azure, carmine, and indigo of the hyacinth, is a sight to be remembered forever. But fashion will have its way, and, as it dictates the formal bed, the question presented for our consideration is: What varieties are best suited for this purpose?

FORMAL BEDS

The first essentials for formal bedding are uniform height and time of blooming. In the tulips, the Duc Van Thols are the earliest to bloom and, except the scarlet, which is a week or so earlier, all bloom at the same period, and are all of uniform height. They come in crimson, rose, yellow, white, and red with a gold stripe. Any of these colors may be selected, but they are much shorter than, and the bloom is not nearly so large as, some of the medium-early sorts. If I were asked to name the best three red, yellow, and white bedding tulips, I would say, in the single varieties—Artus, La Reine, and Chrysolora. Most catalogues describe Artus as a bright scarlet; but it is a medium dark red, at least that has been the writer's experience with it. It grows about 10 inches high, and has considerable demand as a cut-flower.

La Reine is not a pure white, but is slightly shaded rose, which frequently enables it to pass where a pink flower is desired. But the shading is so slight that, when bedded with Artus, it will pass

HOW TO MAKE A BULB-GARDEN

for a pure white except on closer examination. In size of flower and length of stem it is the same as Artus. Chrysolora is a beautiful golden yellow. It is an inch or so shorter than the other two varieties, which makes it desirable for the outer rows. In the doubles, Rex Rubrorum, La Candeur, and Couronne

Tulips for foundation planting

d'Or present strong claims to the distinction of being the best three double bedding tulips.

In the red, white, and blue of the hyacinth I would say, General Pelissier, crimson; Baron Van Thuyll, white, and King of the Blues, make a trio which is hard to beat. When grown in good soil, the spikes are large, round, and full, and make a fine showing. These are all single hyacinths, which are preferable to the double varieties.

SOME GOOD VARIETIES

Where tulips are grown in solid colors, either for the display they make in the garden or for cut-flower purposes, there are many varieties to select from. There are Thomas Moore, orange-color and scented; Picotee, with petals gracefully recurved; Golden Crown, medium tall, with yellow petals edged red; Paris Yellow, late, tall, and handsome; Paris White, the last of the white tulips to bloom; White Swan, medium early, tall, and graceful as its namesake, and fine for cut-flower purposes. Of course, individual tastes differ; but very few, if any, will be disappointed in the above, which are worthy a place in any collection.

The Darwin tulips are among the late bloomers, and are, in the writer's opinion, the finest tulips of all. Coming as they do when other flowers are scarce, their long stems and large, cup-shaped flowers and good keeping qualities make them very desirable as cut-flowers. Usually they are of solid color, although a few sorts are slightly shaded. They are suitable for any location and, when planted in clumps of eight or a dozen among shrubbery, they light up the somber surroundings with a flame of glory that puts to shame the descriptive powers of the English vocabulary.

ODD VARIETIES

Immediately after the Darwins come the Bybloems and Bizarres. These are not admired by everybody, but they are, nevertheless, good tulips. The Bizarres have a yellow background, blotched, striped, and penciled in every conceivable manner

A good tulip-bed

with shades of brown, red, and crimson, giving the petals the appearance of beautiful feathers. They grow tall and stately, and as cut-flowers they keep well. They are among the latest tulips to bloom, and for this reason are most desirable, as they help to bridge the gap between the early spring flowers and the herbaceous perennials and annuals. Bybloems are similar to the Bizarres, except in the contrasting colors. The background of these is white and the markings are various shades of red and purple.

DEPTHS TO PLANT

Tulip and narcissus bulbs should be planted 4 inches deep and from 4 to 6 inches apart. Smaller bulbs, such as the snowdrop, crocus, etc., 2 inches deep and 3 or 4 inches apart; hyacinths, 5 inches deep and 6 inches apart; while the larger bulbs, such as *Lilium candidum*, should be planted 6 to 8 inches deep and a foot apart.

These bulbs do not require to be taken up and reset every year. Every second or third year is often enough; but they should not be allowed to go more than three years, as they would then become too crowded. When dividing, the larger bulbs may be selected for the more prominent parts of the garden, and the small bulbs planted in some out-of-the-way place, where they will get sunshine and rain until they have reached blooming size. A small nursery where these bulbs can be developed is very desirable.

TIME TO PLANT

Now let us review and tabulate the whole collection, with special reference to the planting time. This little inventory will enable us to see at a glance what a wealth of material we have to draw upon, and at the same time will give us a good idea of the month in which they should be planted, and whether they are hardy or tender. Here is the list:

WHEN TO PLANT THE BULBS

May

| Canna | Gladiolus | Tigridia |
| Dahlia | Caladium | Tuberose |

August

Freesia
Oxalis
Lilium candidum*
L. longiflorum and varieties

September

Anemone coronaria	Chinese Sacred Lily	Oxalis
Brodiæa	Grape Hyacinth*	Ranunculus
Calla	Hyacinth*	Snowdrop*
Calochortus*	Lachenalia	Squill*
Crocus*	Narcissus*	Tulip*
Crown Imperial*		

October

| Iris* | Ixia | Nerine |

November

Astilbe*
Amaryllis
Gladiolus
Lilium species*
Lily-of-the-Valley*

*Hardy

SELECT LISTS

The amateur will always be confused by the long lists of varieties in the catalogues, each one described as the perfection of beauty. For all beginners, therefore, a brief list of approved sorts is very desirable, though everyone should experiment for himself and should add some new varieties to his collection annually.

EXHIBITION HYACINTHS

Red and pink:

Fabiola. Pink, striped with crimson; good; large spike.
Gigantea. Extra-large spike; pale rose.
Moreno. The best pale pink.
Norma. One of the best. Uniform rose, with large spike.
Robert Steiger and **Roi des Belges.** Very similar. Deep red and both good.

Blue or lavender:

Czar Peter. Pale blue; one of the very best of its color.
King of the Blues. The best dark blue; large spike and bells.
La Peyrouse and **Pieneman.** Very much alike. Pale blue; enormous spikes.
Queen of the Blues. Pale blue; large and one of the favorites.

White:

Baroness Van Thuyll. White, with pale yellow center; reliable and good.
Grandeur a Merveille. The best blush-white.
La Grandesse. Pure white; one of the largest and most reliable.

Yellow:

King of the Yellows. The largest spike and bells of this color.

Yellow Hammer. The best golden yellow.

The double hyacinths, while fairly pretty if the best bulbs can be secured, are so far inferior to the

A border of hyacinths

single varieties as not to merit a place in a general list.

The single early tulips are larger than the Duc Van Thol varieties, and several weeks later. They combine well with the earliest varieties of large trumpet narcissi, as they blossom at about the same time. The same caution as regards growing in shade after the blossom appears applies to these, as well as to the Duc Van Thol varieties. The number of named varieties of single early tulips is legion. Unfortunately, while good for outdoor culture, many of the finest will not bear forcing. The following list are all reliable forcers, and are generally acknowledged to be the best of their respective colors.

SINGLE EARLY TULIPS

Cottage Maid. Pink-and-white.
Couleur Cardinal. Deep crimson.
Duchess of Parma. Red, edged yellow.
Goldfinch. Yellow.
Keizerkroon. Scarlet, edged yellow; large.
La Reine (Queen Victoria). White, flushed with rose.
Le Matelas. Silvery pink.
Pottebakker Scarlet. Bright scarlet.
Pottebakker White. White.
Prince of Austria. Orange-red.
Proserpine. Carmine-pink.
Queen of the Netherlands. Deep pink.
Vermilion Brilliant. Bright red.
Yellow Prince. Yellow; sweet-scented.

The double tulips follow the single ones in time of blooming, and form a charming class by themselves. The flowers are most of them very sweet-scented, remain in good condition for a long time, and, while not forcing so easily as the single varieties, yet, if the right tulips are selected, are well within the scope of the amateur.

DOUBLE TULIPS

Boule de Neige. White.
Crown of Gold. Deep yellow.
Murillo. White, shaded pink.
Rex Rubrorum. Red.
Tournesol Pink. Pink.
Tournesol Scarlet. Red, edged yellow.
Tournesol Yellow. Orange-yellow.

LATE TULIPS

The late tulip should never be omitted from any garden. The early varieties seem to have a strange preference in the amateur's mind, but the late ones are far superior. They are the finest of all the Dutch bulbs. Some of the best varieties in this list are:

La Reve. Soft rose, shading to apricot at the base; large, globe-shaped flowers.
La Merveille. Magnificent flowers of great size; salmon-rose, shaded orange-red; fragrant.
May Blossom. Pure white, beautifully striped with bright rose.
Miss Willmott. Flowers very large, beautifully shaped and of soft creamy yellow; very fragrant.
Mrs. Moon. Fine late yellow; petals beautifully reflexed.
Picotee (Maiden's Blush). White, penciled and margined with bright cerise, becoming deep pink all over as it matures; lasts long; lovely form.
Retroflexa. Deep yellow; large; petals long, tapering and gracefully recurved.
Scarlet Emperor. Glowing scarlet, with yellow center.
Shandon Bells (Isabella). Bright rose, flaked with white.
Tubergeniana. Bright orange-scarlet, with black center; very large.

DARWIN TULIPS

But for pure joy and unabated glory the Darwin tulips surpass all others. They have good colors, but they are to be admired most of all for their graceful, stately forms. Some good named varieties are the following:

Ariadne. Fiery scarlet.
Bronze Queen. Light yellow; extra large.
Clara Butt. Exquisite shade of soft salmon-pink; a large flower of remarkable beauty.
Flambeau. Brilliant scarlet, with blue center.
Glow. Crimson-scarlet, center blue, margined white.
Gretchen. Large, globular flower of soft blush-pink; very beautiful. One of the very finest.
King Harold. Dark blood-red, shaded maroon.
Kate Greenaway. White, flushed with lilac; very large; late.
La Candeur. Large, globular, white flower, slightly tinged with blush; anthers black.
La Tulipe Noire (The Black Tulip). The darkest of all Tulips; very large.
Loveliness. An exquisite shade of satiny rose-pink.
Madam Krelage. Dark rose, shading to light pink at edges.
May Queen. Delicate rosy pink; large and beautiful.
Old Gold (Yellow Perfection). Golden yellow, overlaid with bronze.
Painted Lady. Soft milky white flowers on purple stems.
Pride of Haarlem. Bright rose, suffused with purple.
Rev. H. Ewbank. Vivid heliotrope, shaded with lilac.
Salmon King. Rich, glowing salmon, with white base.
The Sultan. Glossy black-maroon.
Velvet King. Shining purple; enormous flower.
Zulu. Glossy blue-black; large flower.

HOW TO MAKE A BULB-GARDEN

Other types of tulips not to be overlooked are the Bizarres, the Bybloems, and the Parrots. The Bizarres and Bybloems are large, late varieties, suitable for the border or general garden; the Parrots are earlier and showier, though less dignified. All are well worth having.

NARCISSI

Merging with the tulips as regards blossoming come the large trumpet narcissi, which are the best of all narcissi for display. The smaller varieties can be forced, and in a large collection of bulbs might be included; but, for the ordinary grower who wishes the largest display for the smallest outlay of money, the following will be found by far the most satisfactory:

Empress narcissi, one of the best sorts

Emperor. Very large; pure yellow; one of the finest.
Empress. Yellow trumpet, white perianth; very large and extra fine.
Princeps. Pale primrose-yellow; the earliest of all.

Rugilobus. Golden yellow, with primrose trumpet; very large flower.

Spurius. Golden yellow throughout.

These above, while comprising not a tenth part of the many varieties now listed, have the merit of cheapness as well as reliability.

JONQUILS

The pretty, fragrant jonquils are hardy and willing, and may well be included in any garden collection.

POLYANTHUS NARCISSI

Early Double Roman. Very fragrant; needs staking, and the flowers are not particularly handsome.

Grand Monarque. White, with pale primrose cup; flower extra large; later than the other varieties.

Grand Soleil d'Or. Pure soft yellow, with deep orange cup; stem rather weak and needs staking, but flower very satisfactory; fragrant.

Paper White. The best of all bulbs for water culture; always sure to bloom.

HYACINTHS

Big, buxom, showy hyacinths appeal to every eye, especially the unprejudiced eye of the child. The best Dutch hyacinths have only one real drawback—they are a wee bit expensive. Still, there are many men and women who insist on having them. Comparatively speaking, they are better for forcing than for outdoor planting. Standard single varieties are:

Baroness Van Thuyll. White, with primrose eye; large.
Enchantress. Pale porcelain-blue; large.
General Vetter. Blush-white; large spike.
Gertrude. Good, bright pink; large; good form.
Grand Maitre. Sky-blue.
King of the Blues. Dark blue; large.
L'Innocence. Pure white; immense bells and spike.
Rosea maxima. Delicate rose; fine form.

There are also several very excellent double varieties in different colors. But perhaps the smaller and more delicate Roman hyacinths are even more admired. Good varieties in this class are the following:

Early White Roman. The earliest, as well as the most satisfactory of this class; pure white blossoms. Each bulb produces several spikes.

Light Blue Early Roman. Flowers scanty, but of a beautiful shade of lavender-blue; make a handsome bunch, but do not give a satisfactory display when growing.

Pink Early Roman. Flowers scantier on spike than the white; so pale a pink as to be nearly white; not very satisfactory.

White Parisian. Blossom about two weeks later than the Early White Roman, and are good as a succession. Flowers white, feathery and beautiful, turning to blush as the flowers begin to fade.

LILIES TO THE FRONT

The aristocrats of the garden are the lilies. They are so aristocratic that many persons suppose them unapproachable, undemocratic. Yet what could be more common and democratic than the good old tiger lily? The fact is that several good kinds of lilies can be grown in almost any garden.

A flower-loving friend of mine has a bed of the choicest lilies where only the aristocrats among this charming family are allowed. Many other flowers she has in her garden—sometimes we envy her the great beds of peonies and roses; but when we view the splendors of her lily-bed, envy is lost in admiration.

One fall, seventy-five bulbs of the Speciosum variety were procured, to add to the attractiveness of her bed. The bulbs came late, arriving the twenty-fourth of December, but a place for each bulb had been prepared and marked with a stake, and a heavy mulch had kept the ground from freezing. So, on Christmas day, seventy-one bulbs were planted in the rich loam of the lily-bed. The other four were sent to two friends who had never seriously "considered the lily." I think that, when the crisp, pearly white blooms of *Lilium speciosum album* and the dainty pink *L. speciosum rubrum* unfurled their fragrant petals, there were at least two converts to the charms of the lily.

THE MADONNA LILY

The reliable old *Lilium candidum*, also called Annunciation, St. Joseph's, and Madonna Lily, is the general favorite. These bulbs may be had in August, and should be planted at once—the earlier the better. They will not bloom the following season unless planted early enough to make their growth of leaves in the fall.

The Madonna lily

This is one of the sweetest lilies in existence; its beautiful, snow-white blossoms are the emblem of purity, the world over. It is the lily loved of poet and painter. It is said to be one of the oldest, and is supposed to have been brought to this country by the Pilgrim Fathers, who loved and cherished it even as we do. It blooms in June with the roses and delphinium,—almost too much charm for one short month. But by having a good number of varieties we may enjoy the lily's bloom every month from May to November.

The *L. auratum* is considered one of the finest and most gorgeous of the lily family. It comes to us from the mountains of Japan, and is called the Golden-rayed Japanese Lily. The flower-stalks are usually about 3 feet in height, although they have been known to grow 6 feet high. The blossoms are from 6 to 12 inches in diameter; each petal has a band of golden yellow through its center, and is thickly spotted with carmine. The flowers of this lily vary in color and markings. In some, the spots will be large and of a deep red; in others, they are small and indistinct; but all variations are lovely. The flower lasts a long time before fading. Its odor is very powerful, too much so for the house, but is delightful in the garden. This bulb requires deep planting and a light soil. Unless the conditions are very favorable *L. auratum* will be very likely to deteriorate in our gardens, entirely disappearing in from three to five years; but the bulbs are inexpensive and it pays to grow them.

OTHER GOOD LILIES

The funnel-shaped *L. elegans* is in the class that does well in almost any situation, sun or shade, and is not at all particular as to soil. The cup-shaped blossoms, on stems about 3 feet high, appear in June and July. They range in color from lemon to red. This lily requires absolutely no care, and is showy enough to satisfy anyone.

L. Hansoni is one of the earliest bloomers, its waxy lemon-colored flowers, spotted with crimson, appearing in May.

L. Philadelphicum blooms in midsummer. The showy red flowers shade to lemon in the center, and they are of upright rather than drooping habit. It is a native of several of the eastern states, but grows most abundantly in New York. The small bulb is not set so deeply in the soil as most lilies. I have found it growing only 3 or 4 inches under light leaf-mold. It takes kindly to cultivation. *L. speciosum* is the most daintily colored of any of the family. The beautifully spotted waxy petals are curved, displaying the prominent anthers. *L. speciosum album* is pure white, and the petals have a soft fringe, which adds to its beauty. The whole fragrant flower has a frosted appearance. *L. rubrum* is shaped like the above, but the flower has an exquisite shading of carmine, and is thickly spotted with the same color. *L. Melpomene* is the brightest colored of this class. All the speciosum lilies are perfectly hardy and very free-flowering.

SOME "NEAR" LILIES

My friend's bed of lilies is bordered with funkia, or white day lily. Although these and the hemerocallis are not lilies at all, in any proper popular or scientific use of language, they are so beautiful that they should be included in every collection of lilies. There is the Grandiflora variety, with broad, veined leaves. The white, fragrant flowers are at their best in the evening, and should be planted in a bed near the porch, where they may be enjoyed during the summer twilight hours. The funkias love shade and a moist soil.

Another day lily not allowed in this bed of exquisite beauty is *Hemerocallis fulva*. While there is nothing dainty about this old, tawny orange flower, and it is not considered worthy of a place even in the back yard in a well-regulated border, it needs only the right setting to convince anyone that it is showy, and sometimes very beautiful. I never realized this until I saw them growing on the side of a roadway on the shores of Lake Champlain. The bank sloped to the water's edge, and was covered with the orange blossoms of this day lily. Mingling and growing among the low bushes and so-called roadside weeds, they were positively lovely. How did they come to be roadside tramps? Were they thrown from some garden, and made a home for themselves on this sunny slope; or did someone with imagination have dreams of the effect which might be created with this common flower? I cannot say.

The fact remains that they form a picture, once seen not soon forgotten.

If *Hemerocallis fulva* is considered coarse and unlovely, there is never any question about the beauty of her dainty little sister, *H. flava*, or lemon day lily, which is so profuse with its richly colored

A fine border of hemerocallis

bloom of delicious fragrance. We love to cut their long stems for house decoration, and every bud will develop into a perfect blossom. Furthermore, they make superb garden borders.

CULTURAL REQUIREMENTS

The first and most important thing in the cultivation of the lily is good drainage; for nothing is so sure to injure a bulb as stagnant water about its roots. The ideal soil is rotted sod, leaf-mold, and sand. The bed should be deeply dug, and the soil thoroughly pulverized. If fertilizer be used, it should be thoroughly rotted and placed in the bottom of the bed where the roots will find it, but where it cannot come into contact with the bulb.

The bed should be shaded from the hot midday sun, as its scalding rays injure the beauty of the blossoms, and sometimes cause the buds to blast.

Fall planting is best for all lily bulbs, though spring planting does very well with some kinds, for example, the Madonna lily. They should be set from 8 to 18 inches deep, and from 1 to 3 feet apart, with some good drainage material placed under each bulb.

A SPECIAL BULB-GARDEN

Good results can be secured anywhere with bulbs, but they are so highly specialized in their natural characters that some particular attention may well be given to them in garden designing.

The need is arising more and more for "specialized gardens,"—gardens that shall cater to special horticultural tastes and ambitions. And it is surprising how few people realize what a fund of pleasure is offered, ready to their hand, in even a tiny garden that contains a complete collection of some one of their flower favorites.

One hears always the complaints of "too little space," "too much bother," "too hard to take care of successfully," and last but by no means least, "our summer vacation prevents," offered as excuses for the lack of a garden in many suburban and city homes.

And, for these varied reasons, I believe, are we so often confronted by the ever-prevalent front-yard "variety-shop" type of planting, that strives futilely to be lawn, shrubbery border, and flower-garden, all in one; and which, as even an uncritical public can perceive, too often lamentably fails in its effect.

But to own a garden—and a livable, lovable garden at that—does not necessarily mean that one must be possessed of riches, trained gardeners, a huge quantity of land, or even that one must remain on the premises throughout the summer. The specialized garden offers you beauty and enjoyment in whatever form, or at whatever time of the year, you may prefer.

MISCELLANEOUS BULBS

There are many bulbs, not so well known, perhaps, as the tulip and hyacinth, but which deserve a prominent place in the bulb-garden. Some of these are mentioned in the planting table in the back of this book, with hints as to their treatment.

The ranunculus is an odd-looking bulb, producing flowers of yellow, white and scarlet in early spring. These can be planted late in the fall, about 3 inches deep, care being taken to place the claws on the bulb downward.

Scillas, or old-fashioned squills, are fine for permanent edging, and their rich blue flowers make a beautiful contrast, when mixed with snowdrops. The Star of Bethlehem, or ornithogalum, with green and white flowers, is splendid for naturalizing in the wild garden.

Grape and feathered hyacinths, with small spikes of little blue or white bells are charming when naturalized among shrubbery or grown in a mixed bed.

Montbretias, or tritonias, bloom in the summer, and have brilliant, loose spikes of flowers in shades of yellow and red. These can be treated like gladioli, or can be left permanently in the ground if given a slight protection in winter.

Ixias are curious flowers of the most brilliant colors, and can be treated like tulips, but must be given more protection.

No bulb-garden can be complete without a good show of Spanish iris, which are becoming more popular each year. This species is different from the German iris, and blooms in all imaginable shades from white to deep purple, with a good mixture of yellow.

One of the most gorgeous bulbous flowers is the fritillaria, or crown imperial, with a long stem surmounted by a cluster of rich crimson and yellow flowers. This is perfectly hardy, and can be grown amongst the shrubbery or in the perennial border. It makes an effective center to beds of other bulbs, but is not so good for growing in a bed by itself. It is one of the most conspicuous of all the spring flowers and should be grown more generally than it is.

There are many other bulbs, but most of them are best treated as perennials and planted where they are to remain permanently. In this class are lily-of-the-valley and the anemone, both of which grow in good garden soil without any special treatment.

SEVERAL GOOD QUALITIES

From many types of specialized garden, the spring-flowering garden of bulbs offers itself as one of the foremost in popularity. It fulfils so many demands.

It is a blaze of color just when one's garden desire is keenest, after the bleak, cold days of waning winter; it is easiest of all to care for, as, with the exception of a few, the bulbs are permanent, and increase in beauty from year to year; and, best of all, it can be left to its own devices during the vacation months, with the certainty that its beauty will not be spoiled for the coming flowering season.

A Dutch bulb-garden may be as small as your purse or fancy dictates; but in its designing there are three special points that must be taken into consideration: First, the boundaries used; second, the laying out of walks and beds; third, the varieties and arrangement of the bulbs selected as regards the boundaries. One naturally thinks first of the many beautiful spring-flowering shrubs that, planted in irregular masses or in a double hedge, are used in so many gardens of today. But, in such a garden as we have before us, this is not the best kind of boundary to use. The garden interest should focus in the bulbs themselves, and not be drawn aside from the garden's specialty. A brick or stone wall is one of the best boundaries for such a garden, but is beyond the reach of the average garden-lover's purse. Last comes a hedge of evergreen shrubs, and this is by far the most beautiful and satisfactory method of designating the boundaries of such a garden for general use. Box or holly, where it can thrive satisfactorily, and, in colder climates, fir, or best of all arborvitæ, form a hedge against which the full beauty of the glowing masses of flowers attains its fullest perfection.

PATHS AND BEDS

As to the arrangement of paths and beds, they should be severely formal. In no other type of garden, save perhaps in that abomination known as "carpet bedding," can formality and stiffness of design be used to such good advantage. In a bulb-garden, geometrical arrangements of beds and paths can be used without giving offense, which in other types of gardening would be considered impossible. This, of course, does not apply to the form of spring "wild garden," in which bulbs are naturalized in the grass.

The bulbs should not be too much scattered, but massed boldly as to color and variety; nor should perennial bulbs and bulbs that must be replaced each year be planted together in such a way as to cause difficulty in handling.

In the accompanying diagram, the five central beds around the sun-dial are intended to contain the ordinary early-flowering tulips, that must be lifted and replaced each year. The colors may be selected as desired, but it is preferable to use only one deep color to a bed. A good color scheme would be to have the bed containing the sun-dial of scarlet and scarlet edged yellow, as striking a central note in the garden's color arrangement. The four surrounding beds could be planned as follows:

1. Center, yellow tulips edged and streaked with red; or plain yellow tulips, with a border of white tulips.

2. Center, pale pink tulips, edged with a border of white tulips streaked and splashed with pink.

3. Center, dark red tulips, edged with a border of white tulips streaked and flecked with red.

4. Center lavender, gray, and purple tulips, with a border of white tulips shaded, streaked and edged with lavender.

It will be necessary to select varieties blooming at the same time.

HOW TO MAKE A BULB-GARDEN

DETAILS OF PLANTING

The hyacinths in the four round beds should be of solid colors, edged with white. Pink, lavender, light blue, and yellow are good colors to use. The red may be substituted in place of the yellow.

In the four larger corner beds, double tulips should be used, in much the same color scheme as in the case of the single ones.

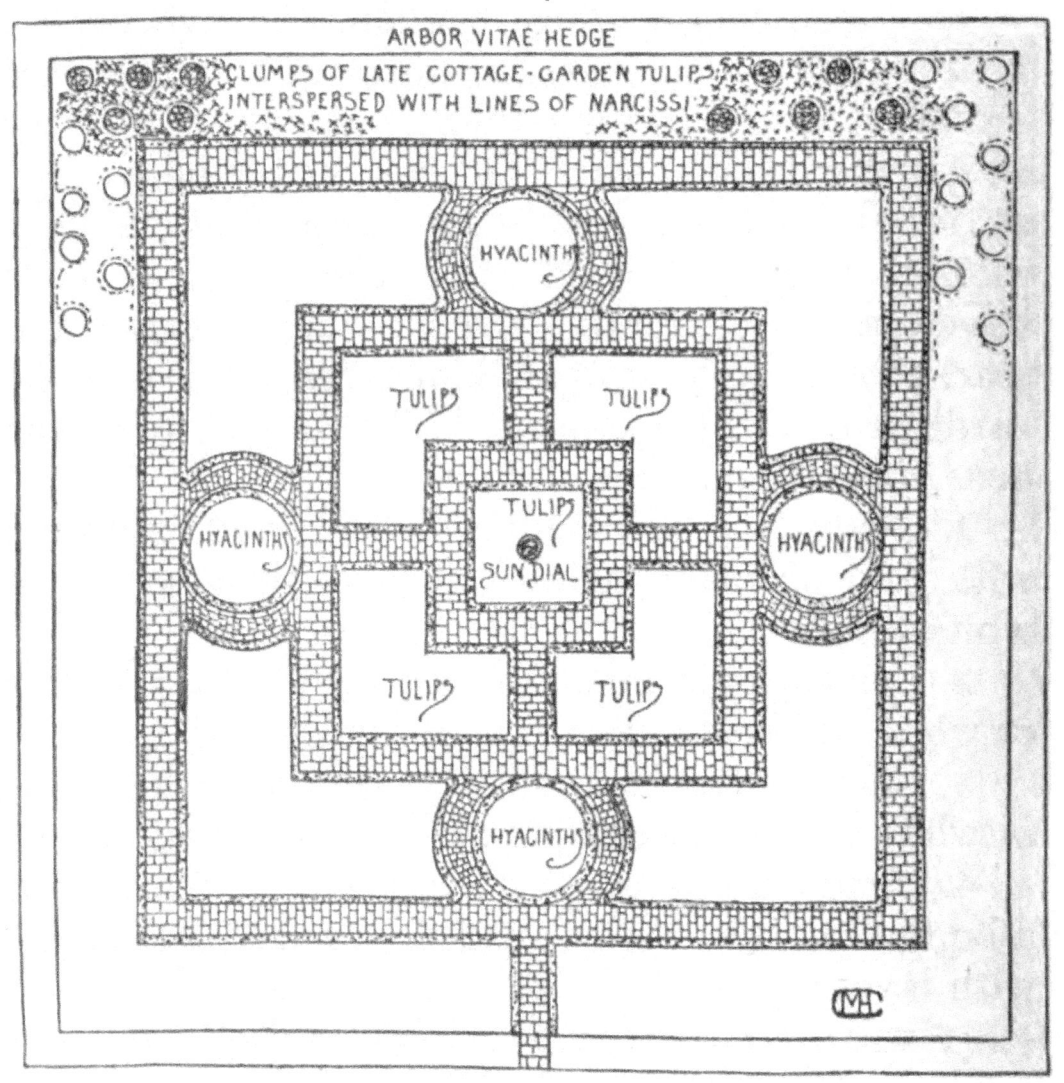

A well-arranged bulb-garden

The outer border nearest the hedge is of late-flowering Darwin and Cottage Garden tulips that do not need to be moved, but increase in number each year. From six to a dozen bulbs should be massed in each clump, and each clump should contain but one variety. Lines of narcissi, containing from fifty to five hundred bulbs in a line, according to the size of the garden and the number of varieties used, should be planted among the tulips, as shown by the diagram. Of course, only one variety should be used in a line.

Finally, a little Dutch bulb-garden is within the reach of all. It can give beauty to a tiny city lot, or can be stretched to cover a large suburban place. Its cost is not prohibitive, neither is the care of it. A few annuals sown when the bulbs are losing their beauty transform it into a little summer annual garden; or, if the family is to be away for the summer, weeds may grow and flourish unmolested, with the certainty that they will cause no harm. Winter frosts will kill them, and clear the ground for the spring's display, with only a little aid from the amateur gardener. And the spring days will bring with them a newer and livelier interest.

PLANTING TABLES

Finally, it seems best to summarize all the foregoing points, along with much other information on the planting and culture of bulbs, in a planting table. Here it is:

A PLANTING TABLE FOR

Common and Botanical Names	Tender or Hardy	Color	Depth to Plant (In.)	Dist. Apart (In.)
Chilian Lily (*Alstrœmeria Chilensis*)	H.	Red, yellow	4	24
Belladonna Lily (*Amaryllis Belladonna*)	T.	Red to white	3	50
Poppy Anemone (*Anemone coronaria*)	H.	Red, blue, white	2	3
Spirea (*Astilbe Japonica*)	H.	White, pink,	2	18
Floral Firecracker (*Brodiæa coccinea*)	T.	Red	2	4
Josephine Amaryllis (*Brunsvigia Josephinæ*)	T.	Red	6	24
Mariposa Tulip (*Calochortus venustus*)	H.	Yellow	8	8
Glory-of-the-Snow (*Chionodoxa Luciliæ*)	H.	Blue	2	2
Meadow Saffron (*Colchicum autumnale*)	H.	Purple, pink, white	2–3	6
Lily-of-the-Valley (*Convallaria majalis*)	H.	White	3	2
Powell's Crinum (*Crinum Powellii*)	H.	Pink	8	12
Spring Crocus (*Crocus Susianus*)	H.	Yellow, purple, white	2–3	3–4
Fall Crocus (*Crocus speciosus*)	H.	Lilac	2–3	3–4
Bleeding Heart (*Dicentra spectabilis*)	H.	Red	2	36
Winter Aconite (*Eranthis hyemalis*)	H.	Yellow	3	6
Eremurus (*Eremurus robustus*)	H.	Rosy	2	48
Dog's-tooth Violet (*Erythronium Dens-Canis*)	H.	Rosy purple, lilac	3	3
Freesia (*Freesia refracta*)	T.	White	1	2
Crown Imperial (*Fritillaria imperialis*)	H.	Red, orange, yellow	3–6	6–8
Snake's Head (*Fritillaria Meleagris*)	H.	Purple and green	2–3	4
Scarlet Fritillaria (*Fritillaria recurva*)	H.	Scarlet	3	6

BULBS INDOORS AND OUT

Time to Force (Weeks)	Blooms Indoors	Blooms Outdoors	Helpful Hints
....	....	July	Bulbs need protection over winter; they must not freeze. Bulbs not ready until November.
6	March	....	Give rich soil and store until flower-scapes show in February in temperature of 45°.
8–10	March	....	Must be given protection over winter. Indoors, plant four roots in a 5-inch pot.
12–14	March	May	Indoors, give 55°. Improved varieties: Gladstone (white), Queen Alexandra (blush-pink).
16	March	....	Brilliant crimson, green-tipped flower, 1½ inches long. Very ornamental.
....	....	July	Prepare ground for planting and mulch till bulbs arrive, or pot bulbs and plant in early spring.
10	March	June	Must be mulched to prevent freezing and thawing during open winters and early spring.
2	Christmas	March	Plant in clumps or in line at edge of borders, or on south side of house.
....	....	Sept.	Scatter in lawn, or plant in clumps in front of border. Flowers without leaves.
21	January	May	For outdoors, buy clumps; for indoors, pips. Store in damp sand in a cool place.
....	....	July	Must be protected by a deep mulch of ashes, and is not hardy in northern states.
2	Christmas	March	Plant six or eight in a 6-inch pan; force in temperature of 55°. Cloth of Gold best variety.
....	....	Sept.–Nov.	Place order early, and plant as soon as received. They will bloom soon after planting.
12	March	May	Buy pot-grown roots for forcing. Force gently and keep plants near the glass.
....	....	March	Prefers a half-shaded situation. Mark the situation, so that bulbs will not be injured.
....	....	May	Must be planted before Sept. 1. Needs well-drained soil and southern exposure. Mulch.
....	....	May	Prefers a light, well-drained soil; excellent for rockeries or massing under shrubs.
16	Christmas	....	Make first planting in August. Succession provided by holding plants in light, cool place.
....	....	April	Flowers have a fetid odor. Grow in clumps. Rich, well-drained soil.
....	....	April	Grown in border or rock-garden, in deep, sandy soil; good cut-flower.
....	....	May	Very different from other fritillarias, and, by some, considered the best.

A PLANTING TABLE FOR

Common and Botanical Names	Tender or Hardy	Color	Depth to Plant (In.)	Dist. Apart (In.)
Snowdrop (*Galanthus nivalis*)..........	H.	White	2	3
Early-flowering Gladiolus (*G. Colvillei*)...	T.	Red, white	2	6
Christmas Rose (*Helleborus niger*)......	H.	White	4	12
Amaryllis (*Hippeastrum spp.*)	T.	Red	2	6
Summer Hyacinth (*H. candicans*)......	H.	White	4	6
Dutch Hyacinth (*H. orientalis*).........	H.	All colors	3–5	5–6
Italian Hyacinth......................	T.	White	1	3
Roman Hyacinth......................	H.	All colors	4	6
Hardy Gloxinia (*Incarvillea Delavayi*)...	H.	Purplish rose	4	18
German Iris (*Iris Germanica*)..........	H.	All colors	3	18
English Iris (*Iris Xiphioides*)..........	H.	Blue, white	3	5
Spanish Iris (*Iris Xiphium*)	H.	Blue, yellow	3	4
African Corn Lily (*Ixia maculata*).......	H.	All colors	3	2
Red-Hot-Poker Plant (*Kniphofia spp.*)...	H.	Red	4	24
Leopard Lily (*Lachenalia tricolor*).......	T.	Yellow, tipped green	1	3
Snowflake (*Leucojum æstivum*)..........	H.	White	4	4
Gold-banded Lily (*Lilium auratum*).....	H.	White	6	12
Meadow Lily (*Lilium Canadense*).......	H.	Yellow, orange, red	6	12
Ascension Lily (*Lilium candidum*)......	H.	White	6	12
Thunberg's Lily (*Lilium elegans*).......	H.	Yellow orange, red	7	12

(68)

BULBS INDOORS AND OUT, continued

Time to Force (Weeks)	Blooms Indoors	Blooms Outdoors	Helpful Hints
3	Christmas	March	Grow in clumps in border; and, for earliest flowers, on south side of walls.
12	March	....	Only early varieties can be forced; others "go blind." Grow in a temperature of 45° to 50°.
2–3	Christmas	Dec.-Mch.	Needs rich, well-drained soil, and should be mulched over winter. Particular as to location.
8	April	....	Summer by plunging outdoors. Store in winter in temperature of 45°. Begin forcing in Feb.
....	....	July	Flowers like snowdrops in spikes. Grow in clumps. Need light, rich soil.
3–4	January	April	Need a rich soil for best results. Do not force before the turn of the year.
4	January	....	Plant three to a 4-inch or six to a 6-inch pan. Later than Romans.
4	Christmas	April	Small-flowering Dutch hyacinths. Give the same treatment and as many to a pot as Italian.
....	....	June	Needs rich, sandy loam, and sunny, sheltered situations in border. Large, trumpet flowers.
....	....	May	Grows in any well-drained soil. Divide frequently to prevent crowding. Good as borders or clump.
6	January	June	Beds must be well mulched. Needs rich, friable loam. Excellent cut-flowers.
8	January	May	Beds must be well mulched. Needs well-drained, sandy soil, and put sand about bulbs.
8	March	June	Indoors, treat as freesias. Outdoors, plant in November. Bulbs must not freeze.
....	....	August	In northern states, take up and store in damp sand in a cool place over winter.
8	March	....	Curiously mottled leaves. Needs treatment of Cape bulbs. Grow in shallow pans near glass.
....	....	May	Prefers half shade. Green-tipped, snowdrop-like flowers in clusters; 15 inches tall.
....	....	August	Very showy, but hard to make live over from year to year.
....	....	June	Easily grown in border, among shrubbery or naturalized in the grass. Well-drained soil.
16	Christmas	June	Effective in clumps, with dark background or in lines along walks in formal garden.
....	....	June	Prefers peaty soil, and either full sun or half shade. Mulch the ground.

A PLANTING TABLE FOR

Common and Botanical Names	Tender or Hardy	Color	Depth to Plant (In.)	Dist. Apart (In.)
Easter Lily (*Lilium longiflorum*)........	T.	White	1	3
Spotted Lily (*Lilium speciosum*)........	H.	Pink, red, white	8	12
Turk's-cap Lily (*Lilium superbum*)......	H.	Orange, red	6	12
Tiger Lily (*Lilium tigrinum*)............	H.	Red, spotted purple	8	12
Grape Hyacinth (*Muscari botryoides*)....	H.	Blue, white	1-3	2-3
Narcissus bulbocodium.................	H.	Yellow	5	3
Narcissus incomparabilis	H.	Yellow, white	4	6
Jonquils (*Narcissus Jonquilla*).........	H.	Yellow	5	3
Narcissus poeticus....................	H.	White	6	4
Narcissus Pseudo-Narcissus...........	H.	Yellow, white	6	5
Paper-White Narcissus (*N. Tazetta*)....	T.	White, yellow	1	3
Guernsey Lily (*Nerine Sarniensis*)......	T.	Crimson	2	6
Arabian Star of Bethlehem (*Ornithogalum Arabicum*)..................	T.	White	1	3
Star of Bethlehem (*Ornithogalum umbellatum*).............................	H.	White	3	6
Bermuda Buttercup (*Oxalis*)..........	T.	Yellow	1	3
Late Peony (*Pæonia albiflora*).........	H.	Crimson, pink, white	4	48
Tree Peony (*Pæonia Moutan*)	H.	White to crimson	4	48
Early Peony (*Pæonia officinalis*)........	H.	White to crimson	4	48
Persian Ranunculus (*B. Asiaticus*).....	T.	Yellow, red	1	3
Calla (*Richardia Africana*)............	T.	White	1	12
Squills (*Scilla Sibirica*)...............	H.	Blue	3	4
Wood Hyacinth (*Scilla Hispanica*)......	H.	Blue, white, pink	3	4

BULBS INDOORS AND OUT, continued

Time to Force (Weeks)	Blooms Indoors	Blooms Outdoors	Helpful Hints
12-14	February	....	The best Easter lily; pot as soon as received, and bury pots until December 1.
....	....	August	Needs light, well-drained soil. Most effective in masses in border, with dark background.
....	....	July	Well-drained soil necessary. Excellent for planting among rhododendrons in beds.
....	....	August	Naturalize near borders of shrubbery or along walls in half-shaded situations.
4	January	April	Naturalize in grass in clumps. Indoors, grown in shallow pans.
4	January	April	Needs well-drained soil and heavy mulch, as it is not very hardy.
3-4	January	April	Many varieties. Divide clumps every five or six years. Grow in clumps in border.
3	January	April	Give well-drained soil. Fragrant. Two to six flowers on stalk.
3-4	January	May	Excellent for naturalizing in lawn or in masses in border. Fragrant.
3-4	January	April	Very fragrant. Plant in masses in border or as an edging for shrubbery.
3-4	Christmas	....	Easily forced for Christmas in temperature of 55° if potted up early.
....	....	Sept.	Plants make their growth during the winter and rest from May to August.
16	....	March	Put six bulbs in 8-inch pot. Leaves need staking. Flowers have black centers.
....	....	May	Naturalize in grass, in partially shaded places, or plant in clumps in border.
8	Christmas	....	Plant six to eight bulbs in 6-inch pot. For earliest flowers, plant in August.
....	....	May, June	Transplant in September when growth has ripened. Single flowers, with bunch of yellow stamens.
....	....	May, June	Does not flower until third year. Needs protected situation and mulch over winter.
....	....	May	Plant singly or in masses. Prefers half-shade. Divide roots every five or six years.
8	March	....	Plant eight or ten in 8-inch pan; treat as Cape bulb. Grow in coolhouse.
....	All winter	....	Needs rich soil and an abundance of water. Thrive best in temperature of 55°.
2	January	March	Best early blue spring flower. Plant in clumps in border. Prefers sandy soil.
2	January	May	Thrives in any soil. Plant in masses in rock-garden or borders.

A PLANTING TABLE FOR

Common and Botanical Names	Tender or Hardy	Color	Depth to Plant (In.)	Dist. Apart (In.)
Wandflower (*Sparaxis*)	T.	Red, yellow	1	3
Autumn Daffodil (*Sternbergia lutea*)	H.	Yellow	6	6
Wake-Robin (*Trillium grandiflorum*)	H.	White	4	6
Montbretia (*Tritonia crocosmæflora*)	H.	Orange, crimson	4	6
Cottage Tulip (*Tulipa Gesneriana*)	H.	All but blue	3	5
Early Tulip (*Tulipa suaveolens*)	H.	All but blue	3	5
Scarborough Lily (*Vallota purpurea*)	T.	Blood-red	1	6

BULBS INDOORS AND OUT, continued

Time to Force (Weeks)	Blooms Indoors	Blooms Outdoors	Helpful Hints
8	March	....	Cape bulb. Plant eight to ten in an 8-inch pan in rich soil. Needs temperature of 55°.
....	....	Sept.	Prefer heavy soil in rather dry situation where they can rest during summer.
....	....	May	Needs a shaded situation and a deep, rich moist soil. Excellent for rock-gardens or borders.
....	....	July	Hardy as far north as Massachusetts and New York, if protected by mulch or coldframe.
....	....	May	The late or May-blooming tulip. Bedding plant or plant in clumps in border.
3-4	January	April	Duc Van Thol the earliest variety. Use as a bedding plant.
....	Sept.	....	Plant one bulb in a 6-inch pot. An evergreen. May be stored in light cellar.

Printed in Great Britain
by Amazon